Something celebrative or immortal under another birdless sky

Peter Ho-cheung Lee

Copyright © 2018 Peter Ho-cheung Lee
ISBN: 978-0-9912975-1-1
Published by Jamii Publishing
San Bernadino, CA
www.JamiiPublishing.com

All rights reserved.

Something celebrative or
immortal under another
birdless sky

Pictures taken down
to envelope my last
song in you

Pictures taken down
from a filthy board
aged with forbidden words
Words too heavy to use
with my decaying tongue
Your smile still lingers
on my wall
fixed loosely by
green magnets
like hibernating ladybirds
waiting to evolve
Pictures taken down
and returned to me
with a single staple still attached
The sting on my ring finger
stays for twenty-eight
seconds longer
than my heartbeat

Pictures taken down
from my screen
and it goes dead
every night I wake it
A sunken face
The first thing there
to remind me of
the gift you offered
You only smile
on Thursdays
and your schedule still
clashes with mine
every weekend
in every aspect you
refuse to tell me
with your eyes

Pictures taken down
from the mirror
above the doll bought
from Japan last summer
The yellowish cattish
stuffed creature
still stares at
my three white hairs
as I found them
protesting
against the sea of
darkness in my
stained distorted reflection
Your closed eyes
burn me wordlessly
as the first time
you gave me the look

Pictures taken down
to bring in the forgotten
moonlight we last had
at the hilltop ruins
where you did not drink
with my bottle, or sit down
for a moment to
comprehend my body,
my body which had
more than language to
speak my desire to dream
with you back to where
these ruins were once
a functional stronghold
against time,
against that which you
did not see in me

Pictures taken down
when you left our country
where you felt warm fingers
run through your veins
like disturbed worms in
clusters on a concrete road
under an expressive cloud formation
You shifted and wiggled and
marked an unnecessary
plot change in my journal
started only yesterday

Pictures taken down
from the hanging
album right in front
of the sliding door of
my balcony
Almost locked you last
time your bare feet
stepped out of my
comfort zone like a
hummingbird mocking
an artificial flower
The thread now bare
So bare that I can't
help but clipping all
of my corpse back up again
to fill out my
rain-eaten sepulcher

Pictures taken down
from my words
I believe I have travelled
with you somewhere
in a layer of the universe
where we both
saw Lagutin's oil-painting
of the sailor boy
sitting still with a
tranquil gaze projecting
into his own
crayon picture
You discuss with me
if it is time to
leave the drawing
behind

Pictures taken down
from that aged
stone wall breathing
through the barred window
The sweat from your back
has soaked through
the blanket so deeply
that even the
wave is unable to
take away my senses
My senses that are
only getting sharper every
second with the
square hollow sponged
on the aged stone wall
so old and fractured and
irrationally hungry
for a touch

Pictures taken down
with my ragged shirt
bearing the mark
from my new wound
It is no longer fresh
as it has stopped
crying since
our eyes met this
morning at the
entrance foyer
Passersby accidentally
witnessed the anti-climax
as if no one were
ever there
No one was knocking
that fucking door in the
first place

Pictures taken down
by force from my
phone in remorse
now for the loss of
the chill morning air
at the memorial park
twenty minutes from
your home
Twenty-eight pictures
and a minute-long
video of you
humiliating the bar
as you muscled up
in fifteen raps
Your shirt cuddled
my shoulder
Light vapor
smoked out of you

as morning dew fell
off the icy metal
You landed on the
crispy leaves
Palm to palm
Your bare chest sheet white
against the blackbirds

Pictures taken down
piece by piece from
your angled face
that afternoon we
whispered
in violet verses
We were in complete
disguise knowing
only cultures from
an extinct civilization
The heat we shared
did more harm than
the unforgiving
slash at the throat
by the autumn storm
I try to remember
when I last folded
your warm pajamas

Pictures taken down
with your pretentious
struggling in a
mock wrestling
last summer colored
with so much
improvised stories
and hilarity
Your half-lifted
vest unfolded
the first rosy mark
that sealed my
promise

Pictures taken down
leaving prominent
room for replacements
that will only come
when you look into
you to find some
skinned body
failing to climb back
up for a gulp of air
The ride to the
mortuary this morning
was too silent
to bear as if
we were all
deafened by the
scream in our own
mistimed
act

Pictures taken down
as nobody wants to
foretell that the rain
tomorrow will cause
the hunters to have geared up
for nothing
No hippos will gather for
their song again waiting
for their wet footsteps
No footsteps will bear
your shoes lodging your
naked feet which
reoccurred whenever I
rubbed my couch till
my back got too warm
to hold your voice
A monologue still
metaphorizes the next rain

Pictures taken down
like fallen wings from
a moon-lit maple

You once yelled I was so rude
as I pulled your right sock
off regardless of how much
work done to clear up
my floor once scattered
with broken glass
from an ill-formed jar
holding my calculated hopes
You once praised the way
I lifted you in that
cellar-like guestroom where
secrets were fed into the
gaps between bible cupboards
You once worded in your dreams
as I left my clothing next to you
and climbed down to the carpet
drowned in your rustling
against the clean sheet as I
milked myself muted
to confirm my own existence
The doomed kiss was
still attached to your right
cheek when I realized
how little air was left
between our lips
Your flawless skin

surfaces from the
glowing waters
three drawers away
This afternoon
I pulled off all
your pictures from the books
of my past lives only
to find a single staple
to draw my blood out
A sole metallic leg of
a mosquito was quite
enough to remind me
of the three thousand leaves
to be collaged
Something celebrative or
immortal under another
birdless sky

Acknowledgements

Thanks must be given to the following literary journals where some of the poems in this chapbook first appeared.

Eunoia Review - Poems on pages 2, 4, 7 and 18, titled as "Heartbeat", "Look", "Sepulcher" and "Something celebrative or immortal under another birdless sky", respectively.

Typehouse Literary Magazine - Poems on pages 9, 11 and 13, titled as "Touch", "Blackbirds" and "Pyjamas" respectively.

ABOUT THE AUTHOR

Dr. Ho-cheung Lee (Peter) is the founding editor of BALLOONS Lit. Journal. His work (poetry/short stories/photography) has appeared in Rattle, *82 Review, Shearsman Magazine, Interpreter's House, The Writing Disorder, The Oddville Press, aaduna, and elsewhere. His poetry was shortlisted in Oxford Brookes University's International Poetry Competition (2016), for erbacce-prize for poetry (2017) and The Proverse Poetry Prize (2017). He teaches English in Hong Kong. [www.ho-cheung.com]

www.ingramcontent.com/pod-product-compliance
Lightning Source LLC
Chambersburg PA
CBHW070050070426
42449CB00012BA/3216